An Eco-School

by Sally Hewitt

Photographs by Chris Fairclough

This edition 2006

Franklin Watts
338 Euston Road
London NW1 3BH

Franklin Watts Australia
Hachette Children's Books
Level 17/207 Kent St, Sydney, NSW 2000

ISBN: 0 7496 6660 9
Dewey Decimal Classification 372.3'57
A CIP catalogue reference for this book is available from the British
Library.

Printed in Malaysia

Editor: Kate Banham
Designer: Joelle Wheelwright
Art Direction: Peter Scoulding
Photography: Chris Fairclough

Acknowledgements
The publishers would like to thank the staff and pupils of Hagbourne
Primary School, Oxfordshire, for their help in the production of this
book. The leaflet on page 16 was reproduced with permission from
the Northmoor Trust. The photographs on page 22 were kindly
supplied by Hagbourne School.

Contents

(Words printed in **bold italics** are explained in the glossary.)

An Eco-School

 The children and staff of Hagbourne Primary School were very proud when they won the Eco-School award for caring for the *environment* two years ago. Now they are even more excited. They kept up their hard work and they have been awarded the flag for another two years.

↑ The school can fly their green eco-flag for two more years.

↑ Each classroom has a notice board, showing the latest environmental news.

Being an eco-school

Being an eco-school means caring for the whole world environment as well as the school environment. Hagbourne pupils know that if they switch off lights and turn down the heating, it will mean they are burning less oil, gas and coal to make electricity. This will mean less harmful gases are given off into the atmosphere.

The school environment

Your environment is what surrounds you. Hagbourne School's environment is a pretty village surrounded by fields. You can see the huge chimneys of the local power station in the distance. The pupils look after their environment inside and outside the school and in their neighbourhood.

Smoke pours from the chimneys of the local power station. →

Inside ...

Inside the school is kept clean and tidy. When visitors arrive they see plants and attractive displays in the main entrance. Every class looks after its own classroom.

We enjoy being an eco-school because we do things that are important.

← **It's the Reception class's turn to water the plants in the main entrance.**

... and outside

It's just as clean and tidy outside as inside. The children try not to bring litter to school, but if they do, they make sure it goes in the litter bin.

Anyone who spots litter puts it in the bin. →

The Eco-Committee

The job of the eco-**committee** is to make sure all the projects are working well and to come up with new ideas. The committee is made up of a representative from every class – the class reps – a school governor, a PTA member and a teacher. The chair is Julia Sargent from the Northmoor Trust, a local environmental organisation that supports the school in its eco-projects.

↑ The members of the eco-committee listen to each other's ideas.

Year 2 ideas

- Buy new plants for the sensory garden.
- Plant more trees in the field.
- Reuse envelopes for dinner money.
- Use both sides of paper.
- Only print one copy of work from the computer - check it thoroughly before printing.

Committee meetings

The committee meets once a week. Julia tells them all the latest eco-news and they discuss how the school can do even better. Each rep brings along a list of suggestions from their class.

Printing just one copy is a good idea because it stops children printing their work, seeing a mistake, correcting it then printing another copy.

Ideas in action

When the committee agrees on an idea, they get busy putting it into action. They decided that the Power Rangers – the team who patrol the school saving **energy** and water – should wear hats and, in no time at all, hats were provided.

Power Rangers are spotted easily in their hats.

← **Dinner money is brought to school in reused envelopes.**

Computer print-outs are only made when it is absolutely necessary. ↓

Questions

Which of year 2's ideas would help the school and which would help the global environment?

What could you do to improve your school environment?

The Power Rangers

The Power Rangers patrol the school turning off taps, switching off lights, shutting windows and doors and looking out for ways of saving energy. The Power Rangers have made up a rap to remind everyone to save energy.

Power Rap

Hagbourne School is the best
To keep our flag
We need no mess
Turn the taps off as you go
To keep our caps we need to show
How to keep those bills low
So turn off that light, turn off that tap
This is the end of our power rap.

The Power Rangers performed their Power Rap to the school.

> When we see the Power Rangers, we remember to turn off lights and taps.

> Everyone in the school should try to save energy.

10

Here come the Power Rangers

Every lunch time the Power Rangers go on patrol.

I can turn off these lights now, everyone's having lunch.

↑ ← The smiling light bulb is a reminder not to waste electricity.

Miss Energy Saver reminds everyone to turn off the taps. ↓

MISS ENERGY SAVER IS MY NAME
SAVING WATER IS MY GAME

SAVE ENERGY
every drop counts

SAVE ENERGY
5 10 15 20 25
TURN IT DOWN

Posters

Posters around the school remind everyone that saving energy at home and at school can help to save the planet.

Green Thinking

Each classroom has a copy of the school's Green Keepers code on their environmental news notice board. It reminds the children of their responsibility to take care of their environment every day.

Help save the world and everything in it by saving energy and avoiding global warming.

Green Keepers

1 Be kind to people, respect each other.

2 Take care in the play area.

3 Walk or cycle to school more often.

4 Keep doors shut.

5 Don't leave taps running.

6 Reduce waste packaging in your lunch box.

7 Keep the classrooms tidy.

8 Use both sides of your paper.

9 Switch off lights.

10 Don't waste food.

11 Put rubbish in a bin.

↑ **These solar panels heat the swimming pool.**

Solar panels

The school takes on major projects that help to save energy. Heating the swimming pool can use a lot of power. **Solar panels** in the roof help to keep the bills down and save energy by using heat from the Sun to warm the water. The Sun provides a huge amount of energy and it doesn't cause **pollution**.

Meter reading

Two Power Rangers take responsibility for checking the gas and electricity *meters* daily. They write down the exact amount of gas and electricity the school is using. It's a responsible job and they need to remember to do it every day to keep an accurate record.

The Power Rangers are the only pupils who can use the key to the meter cupboards.

Questions

Do you think an energy chart could help your school to save energy?

Why do you think solar panels to heat the swimming pool can be a good idea?

All the meter readings for the school holiday were filled in on the energy chart in one very tall column.

Energy chart

The energy chart is filled in so everyone can see the results of the meter readings at a glance. Knowing how much gas and electricity is used every day helps the children to work out why more power was used on one day and less on another. They can then use this information to make improvements.

Recycling

 Some of the things we use every day can be **recycled**. This means they can be changed back into the raw material they are made from. These can then be used again to make something new. Recycling cuts down on waste and saves energy.

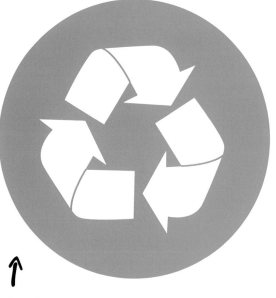

Look out for this symbol on the things you buy. It means it has been made out of recycled material.

Natural materials like oil and aluminium will eventually run out and cannot be replaced. This recycling poster reminds the children not to waste them.

Action plan

The children learn to reduce, reuse and recycle. They reduce the amount of rubbish they throw away. They reuse items and stop them from becoming waste. They recycle things made of paper, aluminium and plastic. Money made from recycling can be used to buy school equipment. Paper, exercise books, furniture and carpets can all be made from recycled materials.

Rubbish!

Recycling paper, plastic and drinks cans means that they won't have to be thrown away. Rubbish is put into big holes in the ground called **landfill sites**. Less rubbish means new landfill sites won't be needed and more of the natural environment can be saved.

The children crush aluminium cans for recycling.

> *Most schools put rubbish in landfill sites. When they are full, more will have to be made.*

Even used postage stamps have a use.

Saving stamps

The children save their used stamps and put them in a collection box in the recycling area. They are taken to the PDSA, an animal charity. They sell the stamps to stamp dealers all around the world and the money goes to the PDSA for their work.

Latest news

We are having a recycling waste paper container delivered soon.
All paper/card/newspapers/magazines (of any colour) will be collected from the school.

The latest recycling news is posted on the notice board.

Go Green Over Lunch

 Green is the colour associated with taking care of the environment. The children try to bring 'green' packed lunches to school. This means not bringing food and drink that comes in packaging that can't be reused and has to be thrown away.

The school is taking part in the Northmoor Trust's 'Go Green Over Lunch' campaign to help reduce waste.

Wash and use again

Hot meals are provided at school and all the plates and bowls, knives, forks and spoons are washed up and used again. Washable containers can be used in lunch boxes, too.

A sandwich box and a plastic bottle can be washed and used again.

Drinks cartons, crisp packets, and foil all end up in the bin.

Question

What would you pack in a 'green' lunch box?

Hungry panda

An ordinary blue compost box for leftover food such as apple cores and orange peel was placed next to the door in the dining room – and hardly anyone bothered to use it! When it was replaced by a hungry panda bin it soon filled up.

↑ **Leftover food needn't be wasted. It can be collected and put on the *compost heap*.**

> **We like the panda bin. It opens its mouth and it's really funny!**

compost heap

To start with, the compost bins in the car park had a few problems. First the exterminator had to be called in to deal with rats, and then the bins had to be secured to the ground because the wind blew them away. Now they are working well. Along with leftovers, dead plants and grass cuttings from the school garden and field are added to the compost bins. Everything rots down and can be dug into the soil to make it richer.

Orange peel, apple cores and teabags make good compost and don't attract the rats. ↑

The Sensory Garden

When an old classroom in the school grounds was pulled down, the children discussed how the empty space could be used to improve the environment around the school. They voted for a sensory garden that would give them beautiful sights and smells all year round.

There are things to see, smell, touch and hear in the sensory garden. →

The children like to find their own marble in the star. ↑

Wishing star

The wishing star is the centre piece of the sensory garden. An artist helped the children to design and make it. When older children come back to visit the school, they can find their own marble in the star and remember the wish they made when they put it there.

Using your senses

Sensory means 'of the senses' and, walking into the garden, the first sense the children use is their sense of smell – the beds are filled with scented flowers and herbs.

The sense of sight enables them to enjoy the colourful flowers and reflections of light and the sky in the mirror. And the sense of touch is useful when looking after the plants. The children respect the sensory garden because they helped to make it and it's their responsibility to look after it.

Peace and quiet

The sensory garden is never too crowded. Only a few children can go in there at a time. A bench provides a quiet place to sit and chat with friends.

In the sensory garden children can escape from the noisy playground. ↗

Travelling to School

 Different ways of travelling to and from school are constantly being discussed. There are lots of things to consider – air pollution caused by cars, how often the buses run, the safety of cycling and how long it takes to walk to school.

↑ Children who live near enough can walk to school.

Cars

Staff and children try to think of ways they can come to school safely, healthily and without causing pollution. If they have to come by car, they could give someone else a lift, for example.

The school is on a busy road. The children who walk to school would like a lollipop man to help them cross the road safely. ↑

Year 6 pupils like to cycle to school on a sunny day.

Cycling

Children in Year 6 can cycle to school if they pass their cycling proficiency test and wear their helmets. There is a bicycle shed in the grounds and somewhere to store helmets and wet weather gear inside the school.

I wouldn't like to walk on rainy days.

Walking bus

The idea of a walking bus is being discussed. It would take a lot of organisation. Every morning, children would wait at points, like bus stops, along the route to school. An adult pulling a trolley for the bags would collect the children and walk them to school.

Most children think the walking bus would be a good idea.

It would be friendly because you can walk with people in different classes.

The morning air would wake you up and you would be ready for school.

You won't be late for school. If people were late it would hold the bus up.

Shovel Brook

The school wanted to start a big environmental project with a five-year plan that would benefit their whole *community*. They didn't have to look very far. A local stream called Shovel Brook had become very overgrown.

↑ **The brook was so overgrown it was difficult to find.**

Letter-writing

The children wrote to the local landowner for permission to do the work, and then wrote to other groups to see if they would like to get involved. They got a very good response.

The students and children discuss ↑ their work.

Dear Landowner

We would like to say how upset we were to see the condition of Shovel Brook. The banks are overgrown and the stream itself has stopped flowing in some places. Over-hanging trees block the natural light.

We are keen to improve this site and would like your permission to carry out this work.

We hope to encourage the community to help us complete our task. With your permission we could achieve our goal.

Yours faithfully,

Class 6/Group C
Hagbourne School

Hard hats

When the work got going, the children wore waterproof coats, wellington boots and hard hats for safety. Students from the local college gave them help and support as they cleared the undergrowth and cut branches.

Now the brook has been cleared, the children pay regular visits to look after it and keep it in good condition.

On the way to the stream, they stop and enjoy the countryside.

They spot yellow marsh marigolds growing by the clear water.

The children aimed to conserve wildlife at the brook and to make it attractive to visitors. So far, they are pleased with a job well done.

 Growing and looking after new plants takes a lot of patience and care. For the Shovel Brook project, the children planted flowers and hedges that grow naturally by water. Young trees were protected by plastic tubes.

Sadly, many of the new plants were vandalised. The children decided not to be discouraged and to plant again.

These are the plants they chose

water iris	cowslip
sedges	primrose
marsh marigold	guelder rose
	spindle
water figwort	blackthorn

Dog owners can pick up any mess made by their dogs and put it in the bin.

Clean path

Local people walk their dogs along the path by the brook. To keep the path clean, the school applied for a grant from the parish council to help to pay for a dog bin.

Interpretation board

Interesting information about a place can help you to appreciate it more. Visitors to Shovel Brook can learn about the plants and wildlife to be found there from a colourful interpretation board. The children measured and mapped the brook and made drawings of plants and the most commonly seen wildlife.

After someone used the board for air gun practice, it has been protected with very tough plastic. ↗

The girls lean over the fence and watch the brook flowing by. ↑

The fence

The brook needed a new fence, and the school decided to make one out of recycled plastic. The material looks like wood and is true to the school's policy of using recycled materials whenever they can. It is very strong and is designed to be vandal-proof.

Questions

What could your school do to improve any local natural areas?

How do you think the children felt when their plants and interpretation board were vandalised?

Outdoor Classroom

Shovel Brook has become a kind of outdoor classroom. It gives the children inspiration for their art and writing and provides material for all kinds of learning.

On our walk we saw a wren going into a pile of logs specially provided for it. You can see wrens all over Britain. They are about 10 cm tall and their eggs are white speckled with red.

When I sit near Shovel Brook I can hear the leaves rustling, water flowing and trickling, and birds singing happy, merry tunes. I love to listen and watch and smell all the things going on.

↑ **The children learn about plants that grow by the water.**

Maths

Maths lessons have included measuring the length and width of the brook so they could draw an accurate map for the interpretation board. They have measured how fast the stream flows and how deep it is, and calculated the volume and area of the water.

← **Children use the metre wheel to measure the path.**

Wildlife

The area around Shovel Brook is teeming with wildlife. With quietness and lots of patience it's possible to see blue tits and jays in the trees, a rabbit hopping by the path or a water vole in the bank. Looking closely at dead wood reveals all kinds of minibeasts living there.

It's exciting to find even the tiniest creatures living in a log.

Everyone has worked so hard to make Shovel Brook an enjoyable, relaxing and pretty place.

The children make sketches of the things they see around them.

Art

The children sit on the bench they helped to install for visitors to enjoy a view of the brook. It is a good place to sit and draw what they see around them. They look carefully as they draw the view, a tree, a plant – or maybe a wild animal if they are lucky enough to see one.

When we visit Shovel Brook we can hear the birds screeching and see the beautiful butterflies fluttering above our heads.

Glossary

Committee
A committee is a small group of people who have been chosen to work on behalf of a much larger group to get a job done.

Community
A community is the people who live together in a neighbourhood.

Compost heap
A compost heap is made up of vegetable material that will rot naturally and can be dug back into the soil.

Energy
Energy is the power needed for doing work. Electricity provides the energy needed to turn on lights, heat water and run machines. We can save energy by remembering to turn off switches and taps.

Environment
Your environment is everything around you. Everyone can help to care for the environment.

Global warming
Global warming is also called the 'greenhouse effect'.
It happens when gases from burning fuels such as oil, coal and gas build up and trap heat in the Earth's atmosphere, gradually warming up the air.

Landfill site
A landfill site is a big hole in the ground used for dumping rubbish. When it is full, the hole is covered over again.

Meter
Gas and electricity meters measure how much fuel has been used.

Pollution
To pollute something is to make it dirty. Pollution happens when the air is filled with dirty smoke or poisonous waste is poured into a river.

Recycle
To recycle something means to use it again. Plastic, glass and paper are all materials that can be recycled.

Solar panels
Solar panels trap heat from the Sun and use it to generate energy. Solar panels do not pollute the environment or waste energy.

Taking Part

Win an award

Hagbourne School has won the Eco-school award for caring for the environment twice running.

Discover what you need to do to win an award for caring for the environment, and work hard to win one for your school.

Work with partners

Hagbourne School works with a local charity that promotes environmental education called the Northmoor Trust.

Find out which charities or organisations – local, national or international – will work with you as partners on your environmental projects.

Plan a local project

Hagbourne School improved the environment for wildlife and visitors by restoring and looking after a local stream.

If there is a neglected pond, stream or any natural site near your school, plan how you can improve it. Invite local people to get involved.

Set up an eco-committee

The eco-committee at Hagbourne School is responsible for making sure everyone in the school helps to look after the environment.

Set up a school eco-committee with representatives from each class – then help them to come up with great ideas.

Index